150
CLASSIC
COCKTAILS

150

CLASSIC
COCKTAILS

First published in 2002 by Hamlyn,
a division of Octopus Publishing Group Limited, 2–4 Heron Quays, London E14 4JP

British Library Cataloguing-in-Publication Data
A catalogue record for this book is available from the British Library

ISBN 0 600 60707 0

Printed in China

10 9 8 7 6 5 4 3 2 1

Notes

The measure that has been used in the recipes is based on a bar measure, which is 25 ml (1 fl oz). If preferred, a different volume can be used providing the proportions are kept constant within a drink and suitable adjustments are made to spoon measurements, where they occur.

Standard level spoon measurements are used in all recipes.
1 tablespoon = one 15 ml spoon
1 teaspoon = one 5 ml spoon
Imperial and metric measurements have been given in some of the recipes. Use one set of measurements only.

US	UK
granulated sugar	caster sugar
maraschino cherries	cocktail cherries
toothpick	cocktail stick
heavy cream	double cream
presweetened cocoa powder	drinking chocolate
confectioners' sugar	icing sugar
pitcher	jug
lemon peel or zest	lemon rind
light cream	single cream
club soda	soda water

SAFETY NOTE The American Egg Board advises that eggs should not be consumed raw. This book contains recipes made with raw eggs. It is prudent for more vulnerable people such as pregnant and nursing mothers, invalids, the elderly, babies and young children to avoid these recipes.

contents

introduction

The word cocktail was first used to describe a mixed drink (spirits with water, bitters and sugar) in an American magazine in 1806. No one is sure where this term originated, although there are several theories, most of them highly unlikely.

Punches, cups and other mixed drinks had been known in Europe centuries earlier, but the Americans developed the art of mixing cocktails and published the first true book on cocktail-making in 1862. Ironically, it was Prohibition, which made it a crime to manufacture or sell alcoholic drink in the the United States from 1920 to 1933, that established the cocktail as a fashionable drink. Tongue-in-cheek names disguised the contents of the drinks sold in illegal bars and clubs as effectively as some of the strongly flavoured ingredients hid the often unpleasant taste of bootleg liquor.

COCKTAIL BASES
Vodka

Flavourless, colourless and odourless, vodka is the perfect partner for other spirits and flavourings – with the additional advantage of leaving no tell-tale signs on the breath. Vodka cocktails are the younger cousins of the classics that had their heyday during the 1920s, and they are now firm favourites in bars and hotels around the world.

Gin

Gin is a clear grain spirit, further distilled with a variety of herb and fruit flavourings, which has been produced commercially for over 400 years. It makes an ideal cocktail base because it blends well with other flavours, whets the appetite rather than dulling it and gives the drinker an instant lift. It is not for nothing that the most famous cocktail of all time – the Dry Martini – is a gin-based drink.

Tequila

Tequila has a bizarre and exotic quality that is missing from the other major spirits. Distilled from the root of the maguey or blue agave, a cactus-like plant, it is Mexico's contribution to the great drinks of the world. It has often been described as having a smooth sharpness. There are several types: tequila blanco, the original version, is colourless while golden tequila (reposado) is aged in oak barrels for up to 11 months. Mezcal is another agave-distilled spirit but with a different style from tequila.

The traditional way to drink tequila is with a pinch of salt. The practice is to lick the salt from between the thumb and forefinger, then knock back the tequila from a shot glass and suck a wedge of lime or lemon. However, tequila also makes a splendid cocktail base.

introduction

Brandy

Although it is better known as an after-dinner drink, brandy is also a great mixer. It is made by distilling wine, fermented juice or mash from any fruit. However, the term is most usually applied to distilled wine made from grapes. The quality of the brandy you choose should depend on the drinks you intend to make. For a party punch, choose a relatively inexpensive bottle as the flavour will be masked by the other ingredients, but if you are making cocktails in which brandy forms the major part, choose a more expensive one. In addition, there are some excellent cocktails which are made with fruit-flavoured brandies such as apricot brandy and cherry brandy. Bénédictine, the sweet, golden brandy-based liqueur, flavoured with a secret mixture of herbs, and Mandarine Napoléon, a brandy-based, tangerine-flavoured liqueur both make fine cocktail ingredients.

Rum

Rum is distilled from molasses and, in some cases, directly from the fermented juices of the sugar cane. There are basically three types of rum – white, golden and dark. The Caribbean produces the best and each island group has its own type. White rum is a popular base for cocktails as it blends easily with a wide range of flavours. Darker rums combine superbly with fruit juices, especially lime, and are perfect for cold or hot punches. Although rum has a strong flavour itself, it combines well with other spirits and liqueurs.

Whisky

Whisky is the oldest known spirit. Its origins are lost in the mists of time but there are official records dating from 15th century Scotland. Whisky also comes from Ireland and from the United States, home of rye and Bourbon whiskey, but aficionados consider Scotch to be the only true whisky. Of all the spirits, whisky is the one least used in cocktails and, when it is used, it is usually found only in the more straightforward cocktails.

Champagne

Champagne is the drink of celebration. Sparkling wines are now made all over the world, but only wines from the Champagne region of northern France can be given the name Champagne.

Champagne and cocktails made with it should be served in long-stemmed flutes or tulip-shaped glasses. These are designed to enhance the flow of bubbles and to concentrate the aromas. When serving, begin by pouring a little into each glass to be filled. Allow the froth to settle, then top up all the glasses to about two-thirds full. This will prevent any Champagne overflowing.

Non-alcoholic cocktails

At parties it is essential to provide a range of soft drinks. Just because cocktails are non-alcoholic, it doesn't mean they have to be dull. With the use of unusual ingredients and exciting combinations, alcohol-free drinks can be just as appealing as those with alcohol.

MAKING COCKTAILS
Bar Equipment
Cocktails are all the better for being made correctly. A well-stocked home bar should contain the following equipment: a cocktail shaker for drinks which are shaken, a mixing glass (also called a bar glass) and a long-handled bar spoon for drinks that are stirred rather than shaken, and a blender for making drinks with ingredients such as fresh fruit and egg white. Also important are a chopping board and a sharp knife, a set of bar measures, a canelle knife for removing spirals of citrus rind, a corkscrew, a lemon squeezer, ice containers and tongs for lifting ice cubes and a supply of tea towels.

Glasses
You can use any number of different glasses for cocktails but there is nothing wrong with serving them in ordinary wine glasses or tumblers. However, the following glasses will come in useful.
• **Cocktail Glass** The classic cocktail glass has a V-shaped bowl set on a tall stem.
• **Old-fashioned Glass** A short, straight-sided tumbler.
• **Highball Glass** This is a tall, straight-sided tumbler most suited to long drinks.
• **Hurricane Glass** A tall glass on a short, dumpy stem. It is shaped like a hurricane lamp.
• **Champagne Flute** This has a long stem and a tall, narrow bowl. It is ideal for serving Champagne cocktails and other fizzy mixtures.

Ice

Ice is one of the most important ingredients in a cocktail. It has two functions: chilling the drink and acting as a beater in the shaker. It can be used in the form of ice cubes, but many recipes call for cracked or crushed ice. To make cracked ice, put the ice cubes into a small plastic bag, fasten the top and then hit the cubes with a rolling pin to break them up a little. To make crushed ice, simply break them up more. Crushed ice cools a drink more quickly than cracked ice, but dilutes it more rapidly. Always use tongs to transfer ice to glasses; using a spoon means that you risk adding water with the ice.

Shaken or stirred?

When mixing drinks, clear drinks are normally stirred in a mixing glass, while cloudy drinks (those containing egg white, cream or fruit juices) are shaken in a blender or cocktail shaker and then strained, ideally into a chilled glass.

SUGAR SYRUP

This is the most practical way of sweetening a drink. Since the sugar is already dissolved it does not need lengthy stirring to blend it into a cold drink.

Put 4 tablespoons of caster sugar and 4 tablespoons of water into a small saucepan and stir over a low heat until the sugar has dissolved. Bring to the boil and boil, without stirring, for 1–2 minutes. Sugar syrup can be stored in a sterilized bottle in the refrigerator for up to 2 months.

vodka

1

Astronaut

Serves 1

8–10 cracked ice cubes
½ measure white rum
½ measure vodka
½ measure fresh lemon juice
1 dash passion fruit juice
lemon wedge, to decorate

Put 4–5 ice cubes into a cocktail
shaker and add the rum, vodka,
lemon juice and passion fruit
juice. Fill an old-fashioned glass
with the remaining ice cubes.
Shake until a frost forms, then
strain the cocktail into the glass.
Decorate with the lemon wedge
and serve.

vodka

Bloody Mary

Serves 1

4-5 ice cubes
juice of ½ lemon
½ teaspoon horseradish sauce
2 drops Worcestershire sauce
1 drop Tabasco
2 measures thick tomato juice
2 measures vodka
salt and cayenne pepper

to decorate (optional)
celery stick, with the leaves
 left on
lemon or lime slice

Put the ice cubes into a cocktail
shaker. Pour the lemon juice,
horseradish sauce, Worcestershire
sauce, Tabasco, tomato juice and
vodka over the ice. Shake until a
frost forms. Pour into a tall glass
and add a pinch of salt and a
pinch of cayenne. Decorate with
a celery stick and a lemon or lime
slice, if you like.

vodka

3

Harvey Wallbanger

Serves 1

6 ice cubes
1 measure vodka
3 measures fresh orange juice
1–2 teaspoons Galliano
orange slices, to decorate

Put half the ice cubes into a cocktail shaker and the remainder into a tall glass. Add the vodka and orange juice to the cocktail shaker. Shake well for about 30 seconds, then strain into the glass. Float the Galliano on top. Decorate with orange slices and serve with straws.

This is a cocktail from the 1960s, named after a Californian surfer called Harvey who drank so many Screwdrivers topped with Galliano that, as he tried to find his way out of the bar, he banged and bounced from one wall to the other.

vodka

4

Vodka Collins

Serves 1

6 ice cubes
2 measures vodka
juice of 1 lime
1 teaspoon caster
  sugar
soda water, to top up

to decorate
lemon or lime slice
maraschino cherry

Put half the ice cubes
into a cocktail shaker.
Add the vodka, lime
juice and sugar and
shake until a frost
forms. Strain into a
large tumbler, add the
remaining ice cubes
and top up with soda
water. Decorate with
lemon or lime slices
and a cherry.

5

Le Mans

Serves 1

2-3 cracked ice cubes
1 measure Cointreau
1/2 measure vodka
soda water, to top up
lemon slice, to
  decorate

Put the cracked ice
into a tall glass. Add
the Cointreau and
vodka, stir and top
up with soda water.
Float the lemon slice
on the top.

vodka

Vodka Gibson

Serves 1

6 ice cubes
1 measure vodka
½ measure dry vermouth
1 pearl onion

Put the ice cubes into a cocktail
shaker and add the vodka and
vermouth. Shake until a frost
forms, then strain into a cocktail
glass and decorate with the
pearl onion.

vodka

Xantippe

Serves 1

4-5 ice cubes
1 measure cherry brandy
1 measure yellow Chartreuse
2 measures vodka

Put the ice cubes into a mixing glass. Pour the cherry brandy, Chartreuse and vodka over the ice and stir vigorously. Strain into a chilled cocktail glass.

vodka

22

Screwdriver

Serves 1

2-3 ice cubes
1½ measures vodka
freshly squeezed orange juice

Put the ice cubes into a tumbler.
Add the vodka, top up with
orange juice and stir lightly.

Variation
*Try substituting
apple juice for the
orange juice and
decorate with a
mint sprig.*

vodka

24

Long Island Iced Tea

Serves 1

6 cracked ice cubes
½ measure vodka
½ measure gin
½ measure white rum
½ measure tequila
½ measure Cointreau
1 measure fresh lemon juice
½ teaspoon sugar syrup (see
  page 11)
Coca-Cola, to top up
lemon wedge, to decorate

Put half the ice cubes into a
mixing glass. Add the vodka, gin,
rum, tequila, Cointreau, lemon
juice and sugar syrup. Stir well,
then strain into a tall glass
containing the remaining ice. Top
up with Coca-Cola and decorate
with the lemon wedge.

vodka

Moscow Mule

Serves 1

3-4 cracked ice cubes
2 measures vodka
juice of 2 limes
ginger beer, to top up
lime or orange slices, to
decorate

Put the cracked ice into a
cocktail shaker. Add the vodka
and lime juice and shake until a
frost forms. Pour into a tall glass,
top up with ginger beer and stir
gently. Decorate with lime or
orange slices.

*This cocktail is one of those happy
accidents. It was invented in 1941 by an
employee of a US drinks firm in
conjunction with a Los Angeles bar owner
who was overstocked with ginger beer.*

vodka

White Russian

Serves 1

6 cracked ice cubes
1 measure vodka
1 measure Tía María
1 measure milk or
  double cream

Put half the ice into a
cocktail shaker and
add the vodka, Tía
María and milk or
double cream. Shake
until a frost forms. Put
the remaining ice into
a tall narrow glass and
strain the cocktail over
it. Serve with a straw.

Black Russian

Serves 1

4–6 cracked ice cubes
2 measures vodka
1 measure Kahlúa
  coffee liqueur
chocolate stick, to
  decorate (optional)

Put the cracked ice
into a short glass. Add
the vodka and Kahlúa
and stir. Decorate with
a chocolate stick, if
you like.

*From the left: Black Russian,
White Russian*

vodka

13

Vodka Martini

Serves 1

4-5 cracked ice cubes
¼ measure dry vermouth
3 measures vodka
green olive or a twist of lemon
  rind, to decorate

Put the ice cubes into a mixing glass. Pour the vermouth and vodka over the ice and stir vigorously. Strain the drink into a chilled cocktail glass, drop in the olive or decorate with a twist of lemon rind.

In some circles this concoction is known as a Kangaroo.

vodka

Vodka Sour

Serves 1

4–5 ice cubes
2 measures vodka
½ measure sugar syrup
  (see page 11)
1 egg white
1½ measures fresh lemon juice
3 drops Angostura bitters,
  to decorate

Put the ice cubes into a cocktail
shaker, add the vodka, sugar
syrup, egg white and lemon juice
and shake until a frost forms. Pour
without straining into a cocktail
glass and shake 3 drops of
Angostura bitters on the top to
decorate.

vodka

Bellini-tini

Serves 1

4-5 cracked ice cubes
2 measures vodka
½ measure peach schnapps
1 teaspoon peach juice
Champagne, to top up
peach slices, to decorate

Put the ice cubes into a cocktail
shaker and add the vodka,
peach schnapps and peach
juice. Shake until a frost forms.
Strain into a chilled cocktail glass
and top up with Champagne.
Decorate with peach slices.

*Use an electric fruit juicer
to make fresh peach
juice or, alternatively,
carefully use a manual
citrus juicer.*

vodka

16

Sea Breeze

Serves 1

5 crushed ice cubes
1 measure vodka
1½ measures cranberry juice
1½ measures fresh grapefruit
 juice
lime slice, to decorate

Put the crushed ice into a tall
glass, pour over the vodka,
cranberry juice and grapefruit
juice and stir well. Decorate with
a lime slice and serve with straws.

Variation
*To make a Cape Cod(der), mix
1 measure of vodka, 2 measures
of cranberry juice and add a
dash of lemon juice.*

*This is one of those drinks that has changed considerably
over the years. In the 1930s it was made with gin rather
than vodka and with grenadine and lemon juice instead
of cranberry juice and grapefruit juice.*

vodka

17

Warsaw Cocktail

Serves 1

6 ice cubes
1 measure vodka
½ measure blackberry-flavoured
  brandy
½ measure dry vermouth
1 teaspoon fresh lemon juice

Put the ice cubes into a cocktail
shaker and add the vodka, brandy,
vermouth and lemon juice. Shake
until a frost forms then strain into a
cocktail glass.

Chi Chi

2 measures vodka
1 measure coconut cream
4 measures pineapple juice
6 crushed ice cubes

to decorate
pineapple slice
maraschino cherry

Serves 1

Put the vodka, coconut cream, pineapple juice and crushed ice into a blender and process until smooth. Pour into a tall glass and decorate with a slice of pineapple and a cherry.

vodka

19

Cosmopolitan

Serves 1

6 cracked ice cubes
1 measure vodka
½ measure Cointreau
1 measure cranberry juice
juice of ½ lime
lime slice, to decorate

Put the cracked ice into a
cocktail shaker and add the
vodka, Cointreau, cranberry juice
and lime juice. Shake until a frost
forms. Strain into a cocktail glass
and decorate with a lime slice.

Blue Moon

Serves 1

5 cracked ice cubes
¾ measure vodka
¾ measure tequila
1 measure blue Curaçao
lemonade

Put half the ice into a mixing glass and add the vodka, tequila and blue Curaçao. Stir to mix. Put the remaining ice into a tall glass and strain in the cocktail. Top up with lemonade and serve with a straw.

vodka

Sloe Comfortable Screw

Serves 1

6–8 ice cubes
½ measure sloe gin
½ measure Southern Comfort
1 measure vodka
2½ measures orange juice

Half-fill a tall glass with ice cubes. Pour the sloe gin, Southern Comfort, vodka and orange juice into the glass and stir well.

Variation
To make a Sloe Comfortable Screw Up Against the Wall, mix the drink as above and top with Galliano. The final part of the name derives from the place in a bar where the tall, slender bottle of Galliano is usually kept.

The name of this drink is an easy way of remembering what goes into it. Sloe for the sloe gin, Comfortable for the Southern Comfort and Screw, short for Screwdriver – vodka and orange juice.

vodka

22

Sex on the Beach

Serves 1

3 ice cubes
½ measure vodka
½ measure peach schnapps
1 measure cranberry juice
1 measure orange juice
1 measure pineapple juice
  (optional)
maraschino cherry, to decorate

Put the ice into a cocktail shaker and add the vodka, peach schnapps, cranberry juice, orange juice and pineapple juice, if using. Shake until a frost forms. Pour into a tall glass, decorate with the cherry and serve with a straw.

vodka

Hairy Fuzzy Navel

6 cracked ice cubes
1 measure peach schnapps
1½ measures vodka
1 tablespoon orange juice

Serves 1

Put the cracked ice into a cocktail shaker and add the peach schnapps, vodka and orange juice. Shake until a frost forms, then strain into a chilled cocktail glass.

Variation
A Fuzzy Navel is made without the vodka.

vodka

gin

Dry Martini

Serves 1

5-6 ice cubes
½ measure dry vermouth
3 measures gin
1 green olive

Put the ice cubes into a mixing glass. Pour the vermouth and gin over the ice and stir (never shake) vigorously and evenly without splashing, then strain into a chilled cocktail glass. Serve with a green olive.

The Dry Martini, which was invented at the Knickerbocker Hotel in New York in 1910, has become the most famous cocktail of all. Lemon rind is sometimes used as a decoration instead of a green olive.

gin

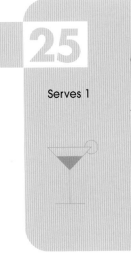

25

Opera

Serves 1

4–5 ice cubes
1 measure Dubonnet
½ measure Curaçao
2 measures gin
orange rind spiral, to decorate

Put the ice cubes into a mixing glass. Pour the Dubonnet, Curaçao and gin over the ice. Stir evenly, then strain into a chilled cocktail glass. Decorate with the orange rind spiral and serve.

gin

French '75

Serves 1

cracked ice
1 measure gin
juice of ½ lemon
1 teaspoon caster sugar
chilled Champagne or sparkling
  dry white wine
orange slice, to decorate

Half-fill a tall glass with cracked ice. Add the gin, lemon juice and sugar and stir well. Top up with chilled Champagne and serve with an orange slice.

'It hits the spot with remarkable precision',
wrote a cocktail book in the 1920s about the
French '75. It still does!

gin

Orange Blossom

Serves 1

4-6 ice cubes
1 measure gin
1 measure sweet vermouth
1 measure fresh orange juice
orange slices, to decorate

Place half the ice cubes in a cocktail shaker, add the gin, vermouth and orange juice and shake until a frost forms. Place the remaining ice cubes in a tumbler and strain the cocktail over them. Decorate the rim of the glass with orange slices.

This is a cocktail from the Prohibition years, when it was also sometimes known as an Adirondack. The orange juice could disguise a hearty slug of rotgut gin.

gin

Clover Club

Serves 1

4-5 ice cubes
juice of 1 lime
½ teaspoon sugar syrup
  (see page 11)
1 egg white
3 measures gin

to decorate
grated lime rind
lime wedge

Put the ice cubes into a cocktail shaker. Pour the lime juice, sugar syrup, egg white and gin over the ice and shake until a frost forms. Strain into a tumbler and serve decorated with grated lime rind and a lime wedge.

If you roll the whole lime around quite hard on a board with your hand, you will find that you get more juice from it.

gin

Crossbow

Serves 1

4-5 ice cubes
½ measure gin
½ measure crème de cacao
½ measure Cointreau
drinking chocolate powder,
  to decorate

Put the ice cubes into a cocktail shaker and add the gin, crème de cacao and Cointreau. Dampen the rim of a chilled cocktail glass with a little water then dip the rim into a saucer of drinking chocolate. Shake the drink vigorously then strain into the prepared glass.

Albemarle Fizz

Serves 1

4-6 ice cubes
1 measure gin
juice of ½ lemon
2 dashes raspberry
   syrup
½ teaspoon sugar
   syrup (see page 11)
soda water, to top up
cocktail cherries, to
   decorate

Put half the ice cubes
into a mixing glass and
add the gin, lemon
juice, raspberry syrup
and sugar syrup. Stir to
mix then strain into a
highball glass. Add the
remaining ice cubes
and top up with soda
water. Decorate with
two cherries on a
cocktail stick and
serve with straws.

Bronx

Serves 1

cracked ice
1 measure gin
1 measure sweet
   vermouth
1 measure dry
   vermouth
2 measures fresh
   orange juice

Place some cracked
ice, the gin, sweet and
dry vermouths and
orange juice into a
cocktail shaker. Shake
to mix. Pour into a
small glass, straining
the drink if preferred.

gin

White Lady

Serves 1

3–4 ice cubes
2 measures gin
1 measure Cointreau
1 teaspoon fresh lemon juice
about ½ teaspoon egg white
spiral of lemon rind, to decorate

Place the ice cubes, gin,
Cointreau, lemon juice and egg
white in a cocktail shaker. Shake
to mix then strain into a cocktail
glass. Decorate with the spiral of
lemon.

Variation
*To make a Pink Lady, substitute
1 teaspoon grenadine for the
Cointreau.*

gin

Juliana Blue

Serves 1

crushed ice
1 measure gin
½ measure Cointreau
½ measure blue Curaçao
2 measures pineapple juice
½ measure fresh lime juice
1 measure cream of coconut
1–2 ice cubes

to decorate
pineapple slice
cocktail cherries

Put some crushed ice into a
blender and pour in the gin,
Cointreau, blue Curaçao,
pineapple and lime juices and
cream of coconut. Blend at high
speed for several seconds until
the mixture has a consistency of
soft snow. Put the ice cubes into a
cocktail glass and strain the
mixture on to them. Decorate
with a pineapple slice and
cocktail cherries. Serve with
straws.

Cherry Julep

Serves 1

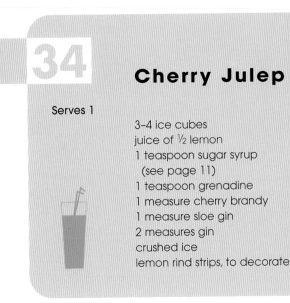

3–4 ice cubes
juice of ½ lemon
1 teaspoon sugar syrup
  (see page 11)
1 teaspoon grenadine
1 measure cherry brandy
1 measure sloe gin
2 measures gin
crushed ice
lemon rind strips, to decorate

Put the ice cubes into a cocktail shaker. Pour the lemon juice, sugar syrup, grenadine, cherry brandy, sloe gin and gin over the ice. Fill a highball glass with finely crushed ice. Shake the mixture until a frost forms then strain it into the ice-filled glass. Decorate with lemon rind strips and serve.

gin

35

Bijou

Serves 1

3 cracked ice cubes
1 measure gin
½ measure green Chartreuse
½ measure sweet vermouth
dash orange bitters

to decorate
1 green olive
piece of lemon rind

Put the ice cubes into a mixing glass and add the gin, Chartreuse, vermouth and bitters. Stir well and strain into a cocktail glass. Place the olive on a cocktail stick and add to the cocktail then squeeze the zest from the lemon rind over the surface.

Chartreuse is made by the Carthusian monks at their monastery near Grenoble, in the French Alps. The recipe is a secret but it is known to contain over 130 different herbs. There are two versions, green which is the stronger, and the weaker but sweeter yellow.

gin

Night of Passion

2 measures gin
1 measure Cointreau
1 tablespoon fresh lemon juice
2 measures peach nectar
2 tablespoons passion fruit juice
6–8 ice cubes

Serves 1

Put the gin, Cointreau, lemon juice, peach nectar and passion fruit juice into a cocktail shaker with half the ice cubes and shake well. Strain the drink into an old-fashioned glass over the remaining ice cubes.

gin

37

Gin Sling

Serves 1

4-5 ice cubes
juice of ½ lemon
1 measure cherry brandy
3 measures gin
soda water, to top up
stemmed cherries, to decorate
  (optional)

Put the ice cubes into a cocktail
shaker. Pour the lemon juice,
cherry brandy and gin over the
ice and shake until a frost forms.
Pour without straining into a
hurricane glass and top up
with soda water. Decorate with
stemmed cherries, if liked, and
serve with straws.

64

Red Kiss

Serves 1

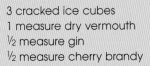

3 cracked ice cubes
1 measure dry vermouth
½ measure gin
½ measure cherry brandy

to decorate
cocktail cherry
lemon rind spiral

Put the ice cubes into a mixing
glass, add the vermouth, gin and
cherry brandy and stir well. Strain
into a chilled cocktail glass and
decorate with the cherry and
spiral of lemon rind.

Sydney Fizz

Serves 1

4–5 ice cubes
1 measure fresh lemon
  juice
1 measure fresh
  orange juice
½ teaspoon
  grenadine
3 measures gin
soda water, to top up
orange slice, to
  decorate

Put the ice cubes into a cocktail shaker. Pour the lemon and orange juices, grenadine and gin over the ice and shake vigorously until a frost forms. Strain into an old-fashioned glass. Top up with soda water, add the orange slice and serve.

Sapphire Martini

Serves 1

4 ice cubes
2 measures gin
½ measure blue
  Curaçao
1 red or blue cocktail
  cherry (optional)

Put the ice cubes into a cocktail shaker. Pour in the gin and blue Curaçao. Shake well to mix. Strain into a cocktail glass and carefully drop in a cocktail cherry, if using.

Although blue Curaçao gives this drink its stunning colour, it is an orange-flavoured liqueur.

gin

Gin Fix

crushed ice cubes
1 tablespoon caster sugar
juice of ¼ lemon
1 measure water
2 measures gin
orange and lemon slices, to
  decorate

Fill a tall glass two-thirds full with crushed ice. Add the sugar, lemon juice, water and gin and stir well. Decorate the rim of the glass with orange and lemon slices.

Fixes are also known as Daisies. They often contain large quantities of fruit or have lavish fruit decorations.

gin

Collinson

Serves 1

3 cracked ice cubes
dash orange bitters
1 measure gin
½ measure dry vermouth
¼ measure kirsch
piece of lemon rind

to decorate
½ strawberry
lemon slice

Put the ice cubes into a mixing glass, then add the bitters, gin, vermouth and kirsch. Stir well and strain into a cocktail glass. Squeeze the zest from the lemon rind over the surface, and decorate the rim of the glass with the strawberry and lemon slice.

gin

Honeydew

Serves 1

1 measure gin
½ measure fresh
  lemon juice
1 dash pernod
50 g (2 oz) honeydew
  melon, diced
3–4 cracked ice cubes
Champagne, to
  top up

Place the gin, lemon
juice, pernod and
melon in a blender
and blend for
30 seconds, then pour
into a large wine glass.
Top up with
Champagne.

Pink Gin

Serves 1

1–4 dashes Angostura
  bitters
1 measure gin
iced water, to top up

Shake the bitters into
a cocktail glass and
roll it around until the
sides are well coated.
Add the gin, then
top up with iced water
to taste.

*Angostura bitters were
developed in the South
American town of
Angostura in the 19th
century. Originally
intended for medicinal
use, they were put into
glasses of gin by the
Royal Navy, thus
inventing pink gin.*

gin

John Collins

Serves 1

5–6 ice cubes
1 teaspoon sugar syrup
  (see page 11)
1 measure fresh lemon juice
3 measures gin
soda water

to decorate
1 lemon slice
1 mint sprig

Put the ice cubes into a cocktail shaker. Pour in the sugar syrup, lemon juice and gin and shake vigorously until a frost forms. Pour without straining into a Collins glass. Add the lemon and mint and top up with soda water. Stir gently and serve.

The Collins is the tallest of the mixed drinks. It is made with a spirit, lemon juice and water. The John Collins, originally made with Holland's gin, was the first. Now there are also the Mick Collins (Irish whiskey), Pierre Collins (cognac) and the Pedro Collins (rum).

gin

tequila

Cadillac

Serves 1

3 lime wedges
fine sea salt
1¼ measures golden tequila
½ measure Cointreau
1¼ measures fresh lime juice
4–5 ice cubes
2 teaspoons Grand Marnier
lime slice, to decorate

Dampen the rim of a chilled cocktail glass with one of the lime wedges, then dip the rim into fine sea salt. Pour the tequila, Cointreau and lime juice into a cocktail shaker. Squeeze the juice from the two remaining lime wedges into the shaker, pressing the rind to release its oils. Drop the wedges into the shaker. Add the ice cubes and shake vigorously for 10 seconds then strain the drink into the glass. Drizzle the Grand Marnier over the top of the drink and decorate with a lime slice.

tequila

Margarita

Serves 1

3 lime wedges
fine sea salt
1¼ measures tequila
¾ measure Cointreau
1¼ measures fresh lime juice
4–5 ice cubes
lime slice, to decorate

Dampen the rim of a chilled cocktail glass with one of the lime wedges then dip the rim into fine sea salt. Pour the tequila, Cointreau and lime juice into a cocktail shaker. Squeeze the juice from the remaining two lime wedges into the shaker, squeeze the wedges to release the oils in the skin then drop the wedges into the shaker. Add the ice cubes and shake vigorously for about 10 seconds. Strain the cocktail into the chilled glass and decorate with a lime slice.

tequila

Floreciente

Serves 1

1 orange slice
fine sea salt
crushed ice
1¼ measures golden tequila
¾ measure Cointreau
¾ measure fresh lemon juice
¾ measure fresh blood orange
  juice
blood orange wedge, to
  decorate

Dampen the rim of an old-
fashioned glass with the orange
slice then dip the glass into fine
sea salt and fill it with crushed ice.
Pour the tequila, Cointreau, lemon
juice and blood orange juice into
a cocktail shaker, shake vigorously
for 10 seconds then strain into the
glass. Decorate with a blood
orange wedge.

tequila

Playa del Mar

Serves 1

1 orange slice
light brown sugar and sea salt
  mixture
ice cubes
1¼ measures golden tequila
¾ measure Grand Marnier
2 teaspoons fresh lime juice
¾ measure cranberry juice
¾ measure pineapple juice

to decorate
pineapple wedge
orange rind spiral

Dampen the rim of a sling glass with the orange slice then dip the glass into the brown sugar and sea salt mixture. Fill the glass with ice cubes. Pour the tequila, Grand Marnier, lime juice, cranberry juice and pineapple juice into a cocktail shaker. Fill the shaker with ice cubes and shake vigorously for 10 seconds then strain into the sling glass. Decorate with a pineapple wedge and an orange rind spiral.

50

Ruby Rita

Serves 1

1¼ measures fresh pink
  grapefruit juice
fine sea salt
ice cubes
1¼ measures golden tequila
¾ measure Cointreau
pink grapefruit wedge, to
  decorate

Dampen the rim of an old-
fashioned glass with some pink
grapefruit juice and dip it into fine
sea salt. Fill the glass with ice
cubes. Pour the tequila, Cointreau
and pink grapefruit juice into a
cocktail shaker, fill with more ice
and shake vigorously. Strain into
the old-fashioned glass and
decorate with a pink grapefruit
wedge.

tequila

Forest Fruit

Serves 1

1 lime wedge
brown sugar
3 blackberries
3 raspberries
2 teaspoons Chambord
2 teaspoons crème de mûre
1¼ measures tequila
2 teaspoons Cointreau
1¼ measures fresh lemon juice
crushed ice
lemon slices, to decorate

Chambord is a black raspberry liqueur and crème de mûre is a blackberry one.

tequila

Dampen the rim of an old-fashioned glass with the lime wedge and dip it into the sugar. Drop two of the blackberries and two of the raspberries into the glass and muddle to a pulp with the back of a spoon. Stir in the Chambord and crème de mûre. Pour in the tequila, Cointreau and lemon juice, add the ice and stir gently, lifting the berries from the bottom of the glass. Decorate with lemon slices and the remaining berries.

Alleluia

Serves 1

¾ measure tequila
½ measure blue Curaçao
2 teaspoons maraschino syrup
dash egg white
¾ measure fresh lemon juice
ice cubes
bitter lemon, to top up

to decorate
lemon slice
maraschino cherry
mint sprig

For maraschino syrup, use the syrup from the jar of maraschino cherries.

Pour the tequila, blue Curaçao, maraschino syrup, egg white and lemon juice into a cocktail shaker, add 4–5 ice cubes and shake vigorously. Fill a highball glass with ice cubes and strain the drink over the ice. Top up with bitter lemon and stir gently. Decorate with a lemon slice, cherry and mint sprig.

tequila

Mezcarita

Serves 1

1 lemon wedge
chilli salt
1¼ measures mezcal
¾ measure Cointreau
1¼ measures fresh lemon juice
4–5 ice cubes
lemon rind spiral, to decorate

Dampen the rim of a chilled
cocktail glass with the wedge of
lemon and dip it into chilli salt.
Pour the mezcal, Cointreau and
lemon juice into a cocktail shaker,
add the ice cubes and shake
vigorously. Strain into the cocktail
glass and decorate with the
lemon rind spiral.

tequila

54

Tequini

Serves 1

ice cubes
3 dashes orange bitters
75 ml (3 fl oz) tequila
2 teaspoons dry French
vermouth,
   preferably Noilly Prat
black olive, to decorate

Fill a mixing glass with ice cubes
then add the orange bitters and
tequila. Stir gently with a bar
spoon for 10 seconds. Take a
chilled cocktail glass and add the
vermouth, film the inside of the
glass with the vermouth then tip it
out. Stir the bitters and tequila for
a further 10 seconds and strain
into the chilled glass. Decorate
with a large black olive.

*This is the Mexican equivalent of a martini, with tequila
replacing the gin and the orange bitters adding an
exotic tang. It is one of the few drinks decorated with
a black olive rather than a green one.*

tequila

Frozen Strawberry

Serves 1

sugar
small handful of crushed ice
2 measures tequila
1 measure strawberry liqueur
1 measure fresh lime juice
4 ripe strawberries
1 teaspoon sugar syrup
  (see page 11)
fresh strawberry, to decorate

Dampen the rim of a chilled cocktail glass and dip it into the sugar. Put the crushed ice into a blender and pour in the tequila, strawberry liqueur and lime juice. Drop in the strawberries, add the sugar syrup and blend for a few seconds. Pour, without straining, into a cocktail glass and decorate with a strawberry.

tequila

Japanese Slipper

Serves 1

1 lime wedge
brown sugar
1¼ measures tequila
¾ measure midori
1¼ measures fresh lime juice
4–5 ice cubes
lime wedge, to decorate

Dampen the rim of a chilled
cocktail glass with the lime wedge
then dip the rim into brown sugar.
Pour the tequila, midori and lime
juice into a cocktail shaker and
add the ice cubes. Shake
vigorously for about 10 seconds
then strain into the cocktail glass
and decorate with a lime wedge.

*Midori is a Japanese melon
liqueur. Combined with tequila
and lime juice, it makes a
delectable drink.*

tequila

Pancho Villa

Serves 1

1 measure tequila
½ measure Tía María
1 teaspoon Cointreau
4–5 ice cubes
brandied cherry, to decorate
  (optional)

Pour the tequila, Tía María and
Cointreau into a cocktail shaker.
Add the ice cubes, shake
vigorously for about 10 seconds,
then strain into a cocktail glass.
Decorate with a brandied cherry,
if you like.

tequila

Tequila Sunset

Serves 1

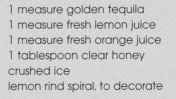

1 measure golden tequila
1 measure fresh lemon juice
1 measure fresh orange juice
1 tablespoon clear honey
crushed ice
lemon rind spiral, to decorate

Pour the tequila into a chilled
cocktail glass, add the lemon
juice and then the orange juice
and stir. Drizzle the honey into the
glass so that it falls in a layer to
the bottom, add the crushed
ice and decorate with a lemon
rind spiral.

tequila

Matador

Serves 1

1¼ measures tequila
¾ measure fresh lime juice
100 ml (3½ fl oz) pineapple juice
1 pineapple chunk
2 teaspoons sugar syrup
 (see page 11)
crushed ice

to decorate
pineapple wedge
lime rind spiral

Put the tequila, lime juice,
pineapple juice, pineapple chunk
and sugar syrup into a blender.
Add a handful of crushed ice
and blend for 15 seconds. Pour
into a highball glass and
decorate with a pineapple
wedge and a lime rind spiral.

tequila

Mexicola

4 lime wedges
crushed ice
1¼ measures tequila
150 ml (¼ pint) Coca-Cola

Serves 1

Put the lime wedges into a
highball glass and crush gently
with a pestle to release the juices
and oils. Fill the glass with crushed
ice, then pour in the tequila and
Coca-Cola. Stir gently, lifting the
lime wedges through the drink.

tequila

61

Tijuana Sling

Serves 1

1¼ measures tequila
¾ measure crème de cassis
¾ measure fresh lime juice
2 dashes Peychaud bitters
4–5 ice cubes
100 ml (3½ fl oz) ginger ale

to decorate
lime slice
fresh blackcurrants or
blueberries

Pour the tequila, crème de cassis, lime juice and bitters into a cocktail shaker. Add the ice cubes and shake vigorously. Pour into a sling glass then top up with ginger ale. Decorate with a lime slice and fresh berries.

tequila

Agave Julep

Serves 1

8 torn mint leaves
1 tablespoon sugar syrup
(see page 11)
1¼ measures golden tequila
1¼ measures fresh lime juice
crushed ice

to decorate
lime wedge
mint sprig

Put the mint leaves into a highball
glass and cover with sugar syrup.
Muddle with a pestle to release
the mint oils. Add the tequila and
lime juice, fill the glass with
crushed ice and stir vigorously.
Decorate with a lime wedge and
a mint sprig.

Tequila Sunrise

Serves 1

5–6 ice cubes
1 measure tequila
100 ml (3½ fl oz) fresh
 orange juice
2 teaspoons grenadine

to decorate
star fruit slice
orange slice

Crack half the ice cubes and put them into a cocktail shaker. Add the tequila and orange juice and shake to mix. Put the remaining ice into a tall glass and strain the tequila mixture into it. Slowly pour in the grenadine and allow it to settle. Just before serving, stir once. Decorate the glass with the star fruit and orange slice.

The Tequila Sunrise is another of the cocktails which was popular during the Prohibition years in the United States, when the orange juice helped to disguise the unpleasant taste of raw alcohol.

tequila

Silk Stocking

Serves 1

drinking chocolate powder
¾ measure tequila
¾ measure white crème de
 cacao
100 ml (3½ fl oz) single cream
2 teaspoons grenadine
4-5 ice cubes

Dampen the rim of a chilled cocktail glass and dip it into the drinking chocolate powder. Pour the tequila, white crème de cacao, cream and grenadine into a cocktail shaker and add the ice cubes. Shake vigorously for 10 seconds then strain into the chilled cocktail glass.

brandy

Tidal Wave

Serves 1

6 ice cubes
1 measure Mandarine
  Napoléon
4 measures bitter
  lemon
1 dash fresh lemon
  juice
lemon slice, to
  decorate

Put the ice cubes into
a highball glass, add
the Mandarine
Napoléon, bitter
lemon and lemon
juice and mix
together. Decorate
with a lemon slice.

*Mandarine Napoléon
is a brandy flavoured
with tangerines.*

Waterloo

Serves 1

1 measure Mandarine
  Napoléon
4 measures fresh
  orange juice
6 ice cubes
orange twist, to
  decorate

Put the ice cubes into
a highball glass, add
the Mandarine
Napoléon and orange
juice and stir together.
Decorate with an
orange twist.

*This drink is named
after the famous
battle.*

Right: Tidal Wave

brandy

Corpse Reviver

Serves 1

3 cracked ice cubes
2 measures brandy
1 measure calvados
1 measure sweet vermouth
apple slice, to decorate

Put the ice, brandy, calvados and sweet vermouth into a cocktail shaker and shake until a frost forms. Strain into a glass and decorate with an apple slice.

Egg Nog

Serves 1

1 measure brandy
1 measure dark rum
1 egg
1 teaspoon sugar syrup
  (see page 11)
3 measures full-fat milk
grated nutmeg, to decorate

Put the brandy, rum, egg and
syrup into a cocktail shaker and
shake together then strain into
a large goblet. Add the milk then
grate some nutmeg on top to
decorate.

Brandy Egg Sour

Serves 1

3 cracked ice cubes
1 egg
1 teaspoon caster sugar
3 dashes fresh lemon juice
1 measure Curaçao
1 measure brandy

to decorate
orange slice
cocktail cherry

Put the ice, egg, sugar, lemon juice, Curaçao and brandy into a cocktail shaker and shake well. Strain into a tumbler. Decorate with an orange slice and a cherry speared on a cocktail stick.

brandy

Brandy Fix

Serves 1

1 teaspoon sugar
1 teaspoon water
2 tablespoons fresh
  lemon juice
½ measure cherry
  brandy
1 measure brandy
crushed ice
lemon rind spiral, to
  decorate

Dissolve the sugar in
the water in a tumbler.
Add the remaining
ingredients and stir.
Decorate with a
lemon rind spiral and
serve.

French Connection

Serves 1

4–6 ice cubes
1 measure brandy
1 measure Amaretto
  di Saronno

Put the ice into an old-
fashioned glass and
pour over the brandy
and Amaretto.

brandy

Brandy Fix

Shanghai

Serves 1

3 crushed ice cubes
1 measure brandy
½ measure Curaçao
¼ measure Maraschino
2 dashes Angostura bitters

to decorate
lemon rind spiral
cocktail cherry

Put the ice cubes into a cocktail
shaker, add the brandy, Curaçao,
Maraschino and bitters and shake
to mix. Pour into a glass and
decorate with the lemon rind
spiral and a cherry on a cocktail
stick.

Frenchman

Serves 1

2–3 cracked ice cubes
1 measure brandy
½ measure green Chartreuse
3 tablespoons fresh lemon juice

Put the ice into a cocktail shaker
and add the brandy, Chartreuse
and lemon juice. Shake to mix
then pour into a cocktail glass.

Brandy Smash

Serves 1

2 mint sprigs
1 teaspoon caster sugar
3 cracked ice cubes
1 measure brandy
splash of soda water

Crush the mint and sugar
together in an old-fashioned
glass and rub the mixture
around the inside of the glass.
Discard the mint. Add the ice
cubes and brandy, then a splash
of soda water.

Variation
*To make a Gin Smash, replace
the brandy with gin. This drink
can also be made with other
spirits such as vodka and whisky.*

brandy

Angel Face

Serves 1

3 cracked ice cubes
1 measure gin
1 measure apricot
  brandy
1 measure calvados
orange rind twist, to
  decorate

Put all the ingredients
into a cocktail shaker
and shake well. Strain
into a cocktail glass
and add an orange
rind twist.

Paradise

Serves 1

3 cracked ice cubes
dash fresh lemon juice
½ measure fresh
  orange juice
1 measure gin
½ measure apricot
  brandy

to decorate
orange slices
lemon slices

Put all the ingredients
into a cocktail shaker
and shake well. Strain
into a cocktail glass
and decorate with
orange and lemon
slices.

brandy

Angel Face

Parisien

Serves 1

crushed ice
1 measure brandy
½ measure calvados
1 measure fresh lemon
  juice
sugar syrup, to taste
  (see page 11)
½ measure Poire
  William (pear liqueur)

to decorate
fruit
mint sprig

Fill a tumbler with
crushed ice, add the
brandy, calvados,
lemon juice and some
sugar syrup to taste.
Pour the Poire William
over the top and
decorate with fruit
and a mint sprig.

Toulon

Serves 1

4–5 ice cubes
1 measure dry
  vermouth
1 measure
  Bénédictine
3 measures brandy
orange rind spiral, to
  decorate

Put all the ingredients
into a cocktail shaker
and shake well. Strain
into a chilled cocktail
glass and decorate
with the orange rind
spiral.

brandy

Monte Rosa

Serves 1

4-5 cracked ice cubes
1 tablespoon fresh
  lime juice
1 measure Cointreau
3 measures brandy

Put all the ingredients
into a cocktail shaker
and shake well then
strain into a chilled
cocktail glass.

Palm Beach Fizz

Serves 1

1 measure apricot
  brandy
1 measure fresh
  orange juice
1 teaspoon Grand
  Marnier
Champagne or
  sparkling dry white
  wine, to top up

Put the apricot
brandy, orange juice
and Grand Marnier
into a Champagne
flute or cocktail
glass and stir well. Top
up with chilled
Champagne or
sparkling wine.

Variation
*Use peach brandy instead of
apricot brandy and Galliano
instead of Grand Marnier.*

brandy

124

Capricorn

4 cracked ice cubes
1 measure Bourbon whiskey
½ measure apricot brandy
½ measure fresh lemon juice
2 measures fresh orange juice
orange slice, to decorate

Serves 1

Put half the ice into a cocktail shaker and add the whiskey, apricot brandy, lemon and orange juices. Shake to mix. Put the remaining ice cubes into an old-fashioned glass and strain the cocktail over them. Decorate with the orange slice.

brandy

Stinger

Serves 1

½ measure white crème de
  menthe
1½ measures brandy
4 cracked ice cubes
mint sprig, to decorate

Put all the ingredients into a
cocktail shaker and shake well.
Strain into a chilled cocktail glass
and garnish with a mint sprig.

Brandy Shrub

Serves 30

grated rind of 2 lemons
juice of 5 lemons
2 bottles brandy
1 bottle sherry
500 g (1 lb) caster sugar

Put the lemon rind and juice into a large bowl or jug, add the brandy and mix well. Cover and leave for 3 days. Add the sherry and sugar, stirring well to dissolve the sugar, then pour the shrub through a sieve lined with muslin.

Brandy Shrub keeps well, so any leftover can be poured into a bottle and stored almost indefinitely.

brandy

Creole Punch

Serves 1

5 crushed ice cubes
1½ measures port
½ measure brandy
2 teaspoons fresh lemon juice
lemonade, to top up

to decorate
1 orange slice
1 lemon slice
pineapple chunks
cocktail cherries

Put half the ice into a cocktail shaker and add the port, brandy and lemon juice. Shake to mix. Put the remaining ice into a goblet, pour the cocktail over it and top up with lemonade. Decorate with the fruit.

brandy

Haiti Punch

Serves 12–15

2 pineapples, peeled and cubed
3 lemons, sliced
3 oranges, sliced
300 ml (½ pint) brandy
300 ml (½ pint) Orange Nassau
   liqueur
2 bottles sparkling dry white wine
orange rind spirals, to decorate

Put the fruit into a large bowl or jug and pour the brandy and Orange Nassau over the top. Cover and chill for several hours. To serve, pour about 1 measure of the brandy mixture into a tall glass, top up with sparkling wine and add some of the pineapple cubes and an orange rind spiral.

The Orange Nassau liqueur can be replaced with Cointreau or Curaçao.

brandy

Penguin

Serves 1

1 measure brandy
½ measure Cointreau
1 measure fresh lemon
  juice
1 measure fresh
  orange juice
splash of grenadine
6–8 ice cubes

to decorate
orange slice
lemon slice

Pour the brandy,
Cointreau, lemon
juice, orange juice
and grenadine into a
mixing glass and stir
well. Fill a tall glass with
ice. Pour the drink into
the glass and
decorate with the
orange and lemon
slices.

Alexander

Serves 1

3 cracked ice cubes
1 measure brandy
1 measure brown
  crème de cacao
1 measure single
  cream
cocoa powder, to
  decorate

Put all the ingredients
into a cocktail shaker
and shake well. Strain
into a cocktail glass
and sprinkle with
cocoa powder.

Pousse Café

Serves 1

½ measure grenadine
½ measure Maraschino
½ measure crème de violette
½ measure Chartreuse
½ measure brandy

Carefully pour each of the ingredients in turn into a tumbler or highball glass to form separate layers. The effect should be like a rainbow of distinct colours.

Maraschino is a colourless liqueur from Italy made with sour maraschino cherries and their crushed kernels.

brandy

133

East India

Serves 1

4–5 ice cubes
3 drops Angostura
  bitters
½ measure pineapple
  juice
½ measure blue
  Curaçao
2 measures brandy
orange rind spiral, to
  decorate

Put the ice cubes into
a mixing glass. Shake
the bitters over the ice
and add the
pineapple juice,
Curaçao and brandy.
Stir until frothy, then
strain into a chilled
cocktail glass.
Decorate with an
orange rind spiral.

Cherry Blossom

Serves 1

1 measure cherry
  brandy
caster sugar
4 cracked ice cubes
1 measure brandy
dash fresh lemon
  juice
dash Cointreau
dash grenadine

Frost the rim of a
cocktail glass with a
little of the cherry
brandy and the caster
sugar. Put the
remaining cherry
brandy and the rest of
the ingredients into a
cocktail shaker and
shake well. Strain into
the frosted glass.

brandy

East India

Monte Carlo Sling

Serves 1

5 seedless grapes
crushed ice
1 measure brandy
½ measure peach liqueur
1 measure ruby port
1 measure fresh lemon juice
½ measure fresh orange juice
dash orange bitters
2 measures Champagne
small bunch of grapes, to
  decorate

Put the 5 grapes into a tall glass
and crush them, then fill the glass
with crushed ice. Put all the rest of
the ingredients except for the
Champagne into a cocktail
shaker and add more ice. Shake,
then strain into the glass. Top with
the Champagne and decorate
with the bunch of grapes.

brandy

rum

Daiquiri

Serves 1

cracked ice
juice of 2 limes
1 teaspoon sugar syrup
(see page 11)
3 measures white rum

Put lots of cracked ice into a cocktail shaker. Pour the lime juice, sugar syrup and rum over the ice. Shake thoroughly until a frost forms, then strain into a chilled cocktail glass.

The Daiquiri was created by an American mining engineer working in Cuba in 1896. He was expecting VIP guests and his supplies of gin had run out, so he extemporized with rum – and created this classic cocktail.

rum

93

Banana Daiquiri

Serves 1

3 cracked ice cubes
2 measures white rum
½ measure banana liqueur
½ small banana
½ measure lime cordial

to decorate
1 teaspoon caster sugar
  (optional)
slice of banana

Put the cracked ice into a
cocktail glass. Put the rum,
banana liqueur, banana and lime
cordial into a blender and blend
for 30 seconds. Pour into the glass
and decorate with the caster
sugar, if using, and banana slice.

94

Apricot Daiquiri

Serves 1

crushed ice
1 measure white rum
1 measure fresh lemon juice
½ measure apricot liqueur or
  brandy
3 ripe apricots, peeled and
  stoned

to decorate
apricot slice
cocktail cherry
mint sprig

Put some crushed ice into a
blender. Add the rum, lemon
juice, apricot liqueur or brandy
and the apricots and blend for
1 minute, or until the mixture is
smooth. Pour into a chilled
cocktail glass and decorate with
an apricot slice, a cocktail cherry
and a mint sprig.

Coconut Daiquiri

Serves 1

crushed ice
2 measures coconut liqueur
2 measures fresh lime juice
1 measure white rum
dash egg white
lime slice, to decorate

Put the ice into a cocktail shaker and add the rest of the ingredients. Shake vigorously until a frost forms then strain into a chilled cocktail glass and decorate with a lime slice.

rum

Strawberry Daiquiri

Serves 1

1 measure white rum
½ measure crème de fraises
½ measure fresh lemon juice
4 ripe strawberries, hulled
crushed ice
strawberry slice, to decorate

Put the rum, crème de fraises, lemon juice, strawberries and ice into a blender and process at a slow speed for 5 seconds, then at high speed for about 20 seconds. Pour into a chilled glass and decorate with a strawberry slice.

This fruity cocktail is especially delicious if you make it with crème de fraises des bois, a wild strawberry liqueur.

Melon Daiquiri

Serves 1

2 measures white rum
1 measure fresh lime juice
2 dashes midori (melon liqueur)
crushed ice

Put the white rum, lime juice and liqueur into a blender with the crushed ice and blend until smooth. Serve in a chilled goblet with straws.

Havana Zombie

Serves 1

4–5 ice cubes
juice of 1 lime
5 tablespoons pineapple juice
1 teaspoon sugar syrup
  (see page 11)
1 measure white rum
1 measure golden rum
1 measure dark rum

Put the ice cubes into a mixing glass. Pour the lime juice, pineapple juice, sugar syrup and rums over the ice and stir vigorously. Pour, without straining, into a tall glass.

Zombies contain all three types of rum – dark, golden and white. The darker rums are aged in charred oak casks while white rums are aged in stainless steel tanks.

rum

Zombie

Serves 1

3 cracked ice cubes
1 measure dark rum
1 measure white rum
½ measure golden rum
½ measure apricot brandy
juice of ½ lime
2 measures pineapple juice
2 teaspoons caster sugar

to decorate
kiwi slice
cocktail cherry
pineapple wedge
powdered sugar

Place a tall glass in the freezer so the outside frosts. Put the ice into a cocktail shaker. Add the rums, apricot brandy, lime juice, pineapple juice and sugar. Shake to mix. Pour into the glass without straining. To decorate, spear the slice of kiwi fruit, the cherry and pineapple with a cocktail stick and place it across the top of the glass. Sprinkle the powdered sugar over the top and serve.

rum

Acapulco

Serves 1

crushed ice
1 measure tequila
1 measure white rum
2 measures pineapple juice
1 measure grapefruit juice
1 measure coconut milk
pineapple wedge, to decorate

Put some crushed ice into a
cocktail shaker and pour in the
tequila, rum, pineapple juice,
grapefruit juice and coconut milk.
Shake until a frost forms, then pour
into a hurricane glass and
decorate with a pineapple
wedge. Serve with straws.

*Whenever a cocktail includes fruit juice, it
always tastes better if the juice is freshly
squeezed. Juice from a bottle or carton is
better than nothing, however, and the
cocktail will still taste good.*

rum

Piña Colada

Serves 1

cracked ice
1 measure white rum
2 measures coconut milk
(see opposite)
2 measures pineapple juice

to decorate
strawberry slice
mango slice
pineapple slice

Put some cracked ice, the rum,
coconut milk and pineapple juice
into a cocktail shaker. Shake
lightly to mix. Strain into a large
glass and decorate with the
strawberry, mango and pineapple
slices.

Coco Loco

Serves 1

crushed ice
4 measures coconut water
1 measure coconut milk
1 measure apricot brandy
1 measure white rum
ground cinnamon, to decorate

Put some crushed ice into a blender and add the coconut water, coconut milk, apricot brandy and rum and blend at high speed. To serve, pour into a coconut shell or goblet and sprinkle with ground cinnamon.

Coconut water is the thin liquid found inside a fresh coconut, whereas coconut milk is made by blending fresh coconut, grated creamed coconut or desiccated coconut with hot water. Both coconut water and coconut milk are sold in cans.

rum

Mai Tai

Serves 1

lightly beaten egg white
caster sugar
1 measure white rum
½ measure fresh orange juice
½ measure fresh lime juice
3 crushed ice cubes

to decorate
cocktail cherries
pineapple cubes
orange slice

Dip the rim of a tall glass into the beaten egg white, then into the caster sugar to frost. Pour the rum, orange juice and lime juice into a cocktail shaker and shake to mix. Put the ice into the glass and pour the cocktail over it. Decorate with the cherries, pineapple and a slice of orange and serve with a straw.

rum

The name of this cocktail is taken from Tahitian and means good – which it certainly is.

Port Antonio

Serves 1

½ teaspoon grenadine
4–5 ice cubes
1 measure fresh lime juice
3 measures white or golden rum

to decorate
lime rind
cocktail cherry

Spoon the grenadine into a chilled cocktail glass. Put the ice cubes into a mixing glass. Pour the lime juice and rum over the ice and stir vigorously, then strain into the cocktail glass. Wrap the lime rind around the cocktail cherry, spear them with a cocktail stick and use to decorate the drink.

Grenadine is a sweet syrup made from pomegranates, which give it its rich rosy pink colour.

rum

Virgin's Prayer

Serves 2

ice
2 measures white rum
2 measures dark rum
2 measures Kahlúa
2 tablespoons fresh lemon juice
4 tablespoons fresh orange juice
2 lime slices, to decorate

Put some ice in a cocktail shaker and pour in the rums, Kahlúa, lemon juice and orange juice and shake until a frost forms. Strain the cocktail into two highball glasses and decorate with the slices of lime.

Kahlúa is a coffee-flavoured liqueur from Mexico.

rum

Bombay Smash

5 crushed ice cubes
1 measure dark rum
1 measure Malibu
3 measures pineapple juice
2 teaspoons fresh lemon juice
¼ measure Cointreau

to decorate
pineapple cubes
lemon slice

Serves 1

Put half of the ice into a cocktail shaker. Add the rum, Malibu, pineapple juice, lemon juice and Cointreau. Shake until a frost forms. Put the remaining ice into a tall glass and strain the cocktail over it. Decorate with the pineapple cubes and lemon slice and drink with a straw.

rum

Batiste

Serves 1

4–5 ice cubes
1 measure Grand Marnier
2 measures golden or dark rum

Put the ice cubes into a mixing glass. Pour the Grand Marnier and rum over the ice, stir vigorously, then strain into a chilled cocktail glass.

Grand Marnier is a brandy-based orange liqueur. It is made by a French liqueur company, hence its presence in this cocktail which comes from one of the French-speaking islands in the Caribbean.

rum

Cuba Libre

Serves 1

2–3 ice cubes
1½ measures dark rum
juice of ½ lime
Coca-Cola, to top up
lime slice, to decorate

Place the ice cubes in a tall tumbler and pour over the rum and lime juice. Stir to mix. Top up with Coca-Cola and decorate with a lime slice. Drink through a straw.

Havana Beach

Serves 1

½ lime
2 measures pineapple juice
1 measure white rum
1 teaspoon sugar
ginger ale, to top up
lime slice, to decorate

Cut the lime into four pieces and place in a blender with the pineapple juice, rum and sugar. Blend until smooth. Pour into a hurricane glass or large goblet and top up with ginger ale. Decorate with a slice of lime.

rum

Mississippi Punch

Serves 1

crushed ice
3 drops Angostura bitters
1 teaspoon sugar syrup
  (see page 11)
juice of 1 lemon
1 measure brandy
1 measure dark rum
2 measures whisky

Fill a highball glass with crushed ice. Shake the bitters over the ice and pour in the sugar syrup and lemon juice. Stir gently to mix thoroughly. Add the brandy, rum and whisky, in that order, stir once and serve with straws.

rum

whisky

Whisky Mac

Serves 1

2–3 ice cubes
1 measure Scotch whisky
1 measure ginger wine

Place the ice cubes in a large tumbler or old-fashioned glass. Pour the whisky and ginger wine over the ice and stir lightly.

whisky

Rusty Nail

Serves 1

2–3 ice cubes
1 measure Scotch whisky
½ measure Drambuie
lemon rind spiral, to decorate

Put the ice into a small tumbler and pour the whisky over it. Pour the Drambuie over the back of a teaspoon on top of the whisky. Decorate the rim of the glass with the lemon rind spiral.

Drambuie is a Scotch whisky liqueur flavoured with heather, honey and herbs. It is said to be made according to a recipe from Bonnie Prince Charlie.

whisky

Algonquin

Serves 1

4-5 ice cubes
1 measure pineapple juice
1 measure dry vermouth
3 measures rye whiskey

Put the ice cubes into a mixing glass. Pour the pineapple juice, vermouth and whiskey over the ice. Stir vigorously, until nearly frothy, then strain into a chilled cocktail glass. Serve decorated with a cocktail parasol and drink with a straw.

whisky

Old Fashioned

Serves 1

2 measures Bourbon
  whiskey
a few drops sugar
  syrup (see page 11)
3–4 dashes Angostura
  bitters

to decorate
orange slice
cocktail cherry

Combine all the
ingredients in a
tumbler and stir.
Decorate with an
orange slice and a
cocktail cherry.

New Yorker

Serves 1

2–3 cracked ice cubes
1 measure Scotch
  whisky
1 teaspoon fresh lime
  juice
1 teaspoon caster
  sugar
1 piece of lemon rind
lemon rind spiral, to
  decorate

Put the ice cubes into
a cocktail shaker and
add the whisky, lime
juice and sugar. Shake
until a frost forms.
Strain into a tumbler.
Squeeze the zest from
the piece of lemon
rind over the surface
and decorate the rim
of the glass with a
lemon rind spiral.

whisky

From the top: Old Fashioned, New Yorker

Whisky Daisy

Serves 1

crushed ice
1 egg white (optional)
½ measure fresh lemon juice
1 measure Scotch whisky
1 teaspoon pernod
2 dashes grenadine
soda water, to top up
lemon rind spiral, to decorate

Put the ice into a cocktail shaker and add the egg white, if using, the lemon juice, whisky, pernod and grenadine. Shake to mix. Pour into a tumbler, top up with soda water and decorate with a lemon rind spiral.

Virginia Mint Julep

Serves 1

9 young mint sprigs
1 teaspoon sugar syrup (see page 11)
crushed ice
3 measures Bourbon whiskey
mint sprig, to decorate

Put the mint sprigs into an iced silver mug or tall glass. Add the sugar syrup, then crush the mint into the syrup using a teaspoon. Fill the mug or a glass with dry crushed ice, pour the whiskey over the ice and stir until a frost forms. Wrap the mug or glass in a table napkin and serve decorated with a mint sprig.

Making the perfect julep is a time-consuming job. Ideally it should be served in a chilled silver mug. Only crushed ice should be used and the mug mustn't be touched during the preparation, otherwise the frost will disappear. If you haven't got a silver mug, use a tall glass instead.

whisky

champagne

Champagne Cocktail

Serves 1

1 sugar lump
1–2 dashes Angostura bitters
1 measure brandy
4 measures chilled Champagne
orange slice, to decorate

Put the sugar lump into a chilled cocktail or Champagne glass and saturate with the bitters. Add the brandy, then fill the glass with Champagne. Decorate with the orange slice.

119

Kir Royale

Serves 1

2 teaspoons crème de
  cassis
chilled Champagne,
  to top up

Pour the crème de
cassis into a chilled
Champagne flute and
top up with
Champagne.

120

Buck's Fizz

Serves 1

60 ml (2 fl oz) chilled
  orange juice
175 ml (6 fl oz) chilled
  Champagne
orange slices, to
  decorate

Pour the orange juice
into a cocktail glass
and add the
Champagne.
Decorate with orange
slices.

*Buck's Fizz can be made in
party quantities in a large
glass jug. Use 250 ml (8 fl oz)
orange juice to a bottle of
Champagne. Be sure to allow
space for the Champagne to
bubble up.*

champagne

182

From the left:
Kir Royale,
Buck's Fizz

Bellini

Serves 1

2 measures peach
  juice
4 measures chilled
  Champagne
dash grenadine
(optional)

to decorate
peach slice
raspberries

Mix all the ingredients
in a large wine glass
and serve decorated
with a peach slice
and raspberries on a
cocktail stick.

Blue Champagne

Serves 1

4 dashes blue Curaçao
chilled Champagne

Swirl the Curaçao around
the sides of a chilled
Champagne flute or wine
glass to coat. Pour in the
Champagne to fill the
glass and serve.

*Curaçao is a sweet,
orange-flavoured liqueur
which can be blue, white
or orange. It comes from
the island of Curaçao in
the West Indies.*

champagne

Apricot Bellini

Serves 6

3 fresh apricots
1 dessertspoon fresh lemon juice
1 dessertspoon sugar syrup
  (see page 11)
2 measures apricot brandy
1 chilled bottle Champagne

Plunge the apricots into boiling water for a couple of minutes. Remove the skins and stones and discard. Put the apricots into a blender with the lemon juice. Process until smooth and sweeten to taste with the sugar syrup. Add the brandy to the purée and divide between six Champagne glasses. Top up with Champagne.

champagne

124

Black Velvet

Serves 1

125 ml (4 fl oz) chilled Guinness
125 ml (4 fl oz) chilled
  Champagne

Pour the Guinness into a 300 ml
(½ pint) glass and carefully add
the Champagne.

125

Emerald Sparkler

Serves 1

1 measure midori (melon liqueur)
3 measures chilled Champagne
melon wedge, to decorate

Pour the liqueur into a chilled
Champagne flute and top up
with Champagne. Decorate the
glass with a melon wedge.

E=mc2

Serves 1

4-5 crushed ice cubes
2 measures Southern
  Comfort
1 measure lemon juice
$\frac{1}{2}$ measure maple syrup
chilled Champagne, to
  top up
lemon rind, to decorate

Put the crushed ice into
a cocktail shaker. Pour
the Southern Comfort,
lemon juice and
maple syrup over the ice
and shake until a frost
forms. Strain into a
chilled Champagne
flute and top up with
the Champagne.
Decorate with a strip of
lemon rind.

Pernod Fizz

Serves 1

1 measure pernod
chilled Champagne,
  to top up
lime slice, to decorate

Pour the pernod into a
Champagne flute and
swirl it round to coat
the sides. Slowly pour
in the Champagne to
fill the glass, allowing
the drink to become
cloudy. Decorate with
a lime slice.

champagne

Whippersnapper

Serves 4

2 peaches, skinned and
  chopped
2 small dessert apples, peeled,
  cored and chopped
2 teaspoons chopped stem
  ginger
1 bottle chilled pink Champagne
16–20 ice cubes
apple slices, to decorate

Put the peaches, apples, ginger
and 2 tablespoons of the
Champagne into a food
processor and blend briefly.
Divide between four ice-filled
tumblers, top up with the
remaining Champagne and
decorate with apple slices.

champagne

La Seine Fizz

Serves 1

1 measure brandy
½ measure crème de fraises
  de bois
½ measure fresh lemon juice
dash orange bitters
2 strawberries, chopped
sugar syrup (see page 11),
  to taste
3 measures chilled Champagne
½ measure Grand Marnier

to decorate
strawberry wedge
mint sprig

Put the brandy, fraises de bois,
lemon juice, bitters and
strawberries into a cocktail shaker
with some sugar syrup to taste.
Shake and strain into a chilled
Champagne glass. Top up with the
Champagne and pour the Grand
Marnier over the top. Decorate
with a strawberry wedge and a
mint sprig.

champagne

192

Bubble Berry

Serves 1

2 raspberries
2 blackberries
½ measure crème de framboises
½ measure crème de mûre
3 measures chilled Champagne
blackberry, to decorate

Crush the raspberries and blackberries in the bottom of a chilled Champagne glass. Add the framboises and the crème de mûre. Top up with the Champagne. Decorate the glass with a blackberry and serve immediately.

Ritz Fizz

Serves 1

1 dash blue Curaçao
1 dash fresh lemon juice
1 dash Amaretto di Saronno
Champagne, to top up
lemon rind spiral, to decorate

Pour the Curaçao, lemon juice and Amaretto into a glass and top up with Champagne. Stir gently to mix and decorate the glass with a lemon rind spiral.

Amaretto di Saronno is a liqueur made from almonds and apricots, first made in Saronno, Italy, in the 16th century.

*Bubble
Berry*

132

Loving Cup

Serves 12

8 sugar cubes
2 lemons
½ bottle medium or sweet sherry
¼ bottle brandy
1 bottle chilled Champagne

Rub the sugar cubes over the lemons to absorb the zest. Thinly peel the lemons and remove as much of the pith as possible. Thinly slice the lemons and set aside. Put the lemon rind, sherry, brandy and sugar cubes into a jug and stir until the sugar has dissolved. Cover and chill in the refrigerator for at least 30 minutes. To serve, add the Champagne to the cup and float the lemon slices on top.

This is an ideal drink to welcome guests on Christmas Day.

champagne

Cardinal Punch

500 g (1 lb) caster sugar
2.5 litres (4 pints) sparkling mineral
water
ice cubes
2.5 litres (4 pints) claret
600 ml (1 pint) brandy
600 ml (1 pint) rum
600 ml (1 pint) Champagne
2 measures sweet vermouth

**Serves
25–30**

Dissolve the sugar in the mineral
water, then pour into a large
punch bowl containing plenty
of ice. Add the remaining
ingredients and stir gently. Keep
the punch bowl packed with ice.

champagne

134

Paddy's Night

Serves 1

3 cracked ice cubes
1 measure green crème de menthe
1 measure Irish whiskey
chilled Champagne, to top up

Put the ice, crème de menthe and whiskey into a cocktail shaker and shake well. Strain into a Champagne glass and top up with Champagne.

135

Valencia Smile

Serves 1

4–5 ice cubes
2 measures apricot brandy
1 measure fresh orange juice
4 dashes orange bitters
chilled Champagne, to top up

Put the ice cubes into a tumbler
and add the apricot brandy,
orange juice and orange bitters.
Top up with Champagne.

Royal Flush

4 cracked ice cubes
1 measure brandy
2 measures Cointreau
2 measures fresh grapefruit juice
1 teaspoon grenadine
chilled Champagne, to top up

Serves 1

Put the ice, brandy, Cointreau, grapefruit juice and grenadine into a cocktail shaker and shake well. Strain into a tumbler or highball glass and top up with Champagne to taste.

champagne

non-alcoholic

137

Cool Passion

Serves 20

500 ml (17 fl oz) orange and
  passion fruit juice
1 litre (1¾ pints) pineapple juice
1.5 litres (2½ pints) lemonade
crushed ice

to decorate
blackberries
mint sprigs

Pour the orange and passion fruit
juice and the pineapple juice into
a large jug. Stir well to mix and
chill until required. Just before
serving, stir in the lemonade. Pour
into glasses containing crushed
ice and decorate each one with
a blackberry and a mint sprig.

non-alcoholic

Tropical Treat

Serves 4

900 ml (1½ pints) natural yogurt
1 large ripe pineapple, peeled
 and roughly chopped
300 ml (½ pint) sparkling mineral
 water
ice cubes
sugar syrup (see page 11)
mint sprigs, to decorate

Place the yogurt, pineapple and mineral water in a food processor and process until smooth, in batches if necessary. Put the ice cubes into a tall jug, then pour in the drink through a very fine strainer. Stir, then add sugar syrup to taste and stir again. To serve, pour into tall glasses and decorate with mint sprigs.

non-alcoholic

Nursery Fizz

Serves 1

crushed ice
orange juice
ginger ale

to decorate
cocktail cherry
orange slice

Fill a large wine glass with crushed
ice and pour in equal measures
of orange juice and ginger ale.
Decorate with a cocktail cherry
and an orange slice speared on
to a cocktail stick. Serve with a
straw. Make to order at a party.

non-alcoholic

140

Tenderberry

Serves 1

6–8 strawberries
1 measure grenadine
1 measure double cream
crushed ice
1 measure ginger ale
pinch of ground ginger
strawberry, to decorate
(optional)

Place the strawberries, grenadine
and cream in a food processor
with some crushed ice and
process for 30 seconds. Pour into
a glass. Add the ginger ale and
stir. Sprinkle a little ground ginger
on top and decorate with a
strawberry, if you like.

Variation
*Raspberries make a delicious
alternative in this recipe, but it is
advisable to strain the drink after
blending to remove the pips.*

non-alcoholic

208

141

Banana Shake

Serves 2

1 ripe banana, chopped
juice of 1 orange
1 teaspoon clear honey
300 ml (½ pint) full-fat milk
8 ice cubes
pinch of ground cinnamon

Place the banana, orange juice, honey and milk in a food processor and process until smooth. Divide the ice between two tall glasses, pour in the drink and sprinkle with cinnamon.

Variation
To make a Mango Shake, substitute a ripe mango for the banana. Peel the mango and remove the stone before processing. You may wish to leave out the honey if the mango is very sweet.

non-alcoholic

Bugs Bunny

Serves 1

4–6 ice cubes
50 ml (2 fl oz) carrot juice
50 ml (2 fl oz) orange juice
dash Tabasco
1 celery stick, to decorate

Put the ice cubes into a tumbler,
pour in the carrot juice and
orange juice then add a dash of
Tabasco and decorate with a
celery stick.

non-alcoholic

Garden Cooler

Serves 1

crushed ice
150 ml (¼ pint) tomato
  juice
25 g (1 oz) cucumber,
  peeled
2 dashes fresh
  lemon juice
2 dashes
  Worcestershire sauce
salt and pepper
cucumber slice, to
  decorate

Put a little crushed ice
into a food processor.
Add the tomato juice,
cucumber, lemon
juice, Worcestershire
sauce and salt and
pepper to taste and
process well. Pour the
drink into a cocktail
glass and decorate
with a cucumber slice.

Guavarama

Serves 1

crushed ice
200 ml (7 fl oz) guava
  juice
2 teaspoons lime juice
4 teaspoons
blackcurrant syrup
5 dashes rum essence
melon slice, to
  decorate

Put some crushed ice
into a food processor
and add the guava
juice, lime juice,
blackcurrant syrup
and rum essence.
Process thoroughly
then strain into a
chilled cocktail glass
and decorate with a
melon slice.

non-alcoholic

145

Orange Berry Crush

Serves 2-3

200 ml (7 fl oz) cranberry juice
100 ml (3½ fl oz) orange juice
250 ml (8 fl oz) raspberries
3 scoops orange sorbet, plus
  extra to decorate
sugar syrup (see page 11)
  (optional)

Put the cranberry juice, orange juice, raspberries and orange sorbet into a food processor and process until frothy. Taste and add sugar syrup, if required.
Serve in cocktail glasses, adding an extra scoop of sorbet to each one.

non-alcoholic

Appleade

Serves 3

2 large dessert apples
600 ml (1 pint) boiling water
½ teaspoon sugar
ice cubes
apple slices, to decorate

Chop the apples and place in a bowl. Pour the boiling water over the apples and add the sugar. Leave to stand for 10 minutes, then strain into a jug and allow to cool. Put several ice cubes into three tall glasses, pour in the appleade and decorate with apple slices. Serve with straws.

Carib Cream

Serves 1

1 small banana, chopped
1 measure fresh lemon juice
1 measure full-fat milk
crushed ice
1 teaspoon finely chopped
  walnuts

Place the banana, lemon juice
and milk in a food processor with
some crushed ice and process on
maximum speed until smooth.
Pour into a cocktail glass and
sprinkle the chopped walnuts on
top just before serving.

non-alcoholic

148

Virgin Colada

Serves 1

1 measure coconut cream
2 measures pineapple juice
crushed ice
pineapple wedge, to decorate

Place the coconut cream, pineapple juice and crushed ice in a food processor and process, or shake in a cocktail shaker. Pour into a tall glass and decorate with a pineapple wedge. Serve with a straw.

149

St Clements

Serves 1

4 ice cubes
2 measures fresh orange juice
2 measures bitter lemon
orange slice, to decorate

Put the ice cubes in a tumbler,
pour in the orange juice and
bitter lemon and stir together.
Decorate with the orange slice.

non-alcoholic

Jersey Lily

150 ml (¼ pint) sparkling
  apple juice
2 dashes Angostura bitters
¼ teaspoon caster sugar
ice cubes
cocktail cherry, to decorate

Put the apple juice, bitters, sugar
and ice cubes in a cocktail
shaker. Shake well, then strain into
a wine glass. Decorate with a
cocktail cherry.

Variation
*Sparkling grape juice, either red
or white, makes a refreshing
substitute for the apple juice.*

non-alcoholic

index

acknowledgements

in Source Order:
Octopus Publishing Group
Limited/Jean Cazals 1, 4 top, 6 centre
bottom/Neil Mersh 12–13 background,
19, 27, 33, 39, 44–45 background, 45
centre, 47, 53, 65, 67, 107 top, 135, 139
top, 139 centre, 141, 143, 147, 157, 163,
166–167, 167 top, 167 bottom, 171, 173,
177, 179 centre, 181/William Reavell
2–3, 4 centre bottom, 4 centre top, 4
bottom, 4–5, 6 top, 6 centre top, 6
bottom, 6–7, 8–9, 10–11, 13 top, 13
centre, 13 bottom, 15, 17, 23, 29, 35, 45
top, 45 bottom, 49, 55, 59, 61, 71, 74–75
background, 75 top, 75 centre, 75
bottom, 77, 81, 83, 85, 89, 93, 95, 99, 101,
103, 104, 106 background, 107 centre,
107 bottom, 109, 111, 115, 117, 121, 123,
127, 131, 137, 138–139, 139 bottom,
151, 153, 159, 167 centre, 175, 178–179,
179, 179 bottom, 183, 186, 189, 193, 195,
199, 202 centre, 202–203, 203 top, 203
bottom, 205, 209, 213, 215, 219

commissioning editor: **Sarah Ford**
editor: **Joanna Smith**
senior designer: **Joanna Bennett**
designer: **Bill Mason**
production manager: **Louise Hall**